Anonymus

The Irish princess

And other legendary and colonial tales

Anonymus

The Irish princess
And other legendary and colonial tales

ISBN/EAN: 9783741194559

Manufactured in Europe, USA, Canada, Australia, Japa

Cover: Foto ©Andreas Hilbeck / pixelio.de

Manufactured and distributed by brebook publishing software (www.brebook.com)

Anonymus

The Irish princess

THE

IRISH PRINCESS:

AND OTHER

LEGENDARY AND COLONIAL TALES.

BY THE AUTHOR OF
"TRADITIONS OF TIROL."

With an Illustration by E. H. Corbould.

BALTIMORE:
KELLY, PIET AND COMPANY,
174 & 176 BALTIMORE STREET.
1871.

THE IRISH PRINCESS	9
EL CLAVEL	30
THE ILL-TEMPERED PRINCESS	38
TURIAN AND FLORETA	58
THE PEDRO JIMENEZ GRAPE	92
MOORISH REMNANTS — ISSY-BEN-ARAN . . .	107
MOORISH REMNANTS — MÓSTAFA ALVILÁ . . .	113
MOORISH REMNANTS — THE EMIR IN SEARCH OF AN EYE	118
MOORISH REMNANTS — YUSSUF'S FRIEND . . .	122
MOORISH REMNANTS — THE SULTANA'S PERFUMER-IN-CHIEF	126
ARAUCANIA THE INDOMITABLE	128
ARAUCANIA — TEGUALDA	143
ARAUCANIA — FITON'S CAVE	159
RAGUEL; OR, THE JEWESS OF TOLEDO . . .	177

VOL. II.

THE IRISH PRINCESS.*

I WAS born in Venice the renowned. When I had completed my twenty Aprils, my father called me to him one day, and said to me, "Dear son, I have overflowing wealth of possessions, and in silver and gold twenty thousand doubloons fully told; you are my only heir, and I am infirm and stricken in years. I am think-

* Though neither of the persons in this piece are Spanish, nor the scene laid in the Peninsula, it is thoroughly Spanish in character, and the subject of one or two popular ballads, and several dramas, by the best authors.

ing of selling the good ship, that even now lies anchored in port."

To which I replied, "Father and lord, observe, the possessions, silver and gold, may all in an instant be reduced to nothing. But freight the good ship now with rich merchandise and wares which shall profit in exchange."

A few days after this, I sailed forth in the good ship, well freighted with precious stores; her linen sails filled out with the soft wind, and her keel ploughing the *berdinegros** waters of the crystal main.

Thus to Tunis we came, where my affairs succeeded prosperously. My merchandise was all disposed of to great advantage in a short time, and before leaving the port

* Dark-green (*lit.* black-green).

I wandered forth to see the town. Passing by one of the great public squares, I saw some Turkish sentinels walking up and down, guarding a dead body; I addressed them, asking why they did not inter it.

"Because," said they, "he was of the Christian people, and in his days of life traded with his ship, wherefore a Turk of great consideration in our city, and a friend of his, entrusted to him a thousand ducats in silver, with which he bought great provision of cloth, and sent his servants to trade with it, while he remained in Tunis. The ship left the port with a prosperous wind, but before four days were out, a *balandra** came in, bearing the news that

---

* A small coasting-boat, carrying only a boom sail.

the ship had been overtaken by a tempest, and all the merchandise had gone down into the boiling deep. With that the Christian merchant was so overcome, that he fainted and fell down dead, and we hold his body in bail for the thousand ducats he owed the Turk."

To which I replied, "I will pay the sum you have named." And then, taking the body on my shoulders, I carried it to the church of Serafic Francis, which there is in Tunis, to give it burial, and paid the stipend of the priest who should say a hundred masses for the soul's rest. Then I returned to pay the debt to the Turk. .

Scarcely had I passed the threshold of his house, when I heard the sound of great wailing and lamentation, as of one taking leave of life.

So I turned and asked two turbaned renegades who stood in waiting, what meant the wail. And they said, "There came to Tunis a female slave, a captive Christian, causing envy to all the womanhood of this place, so beauteously had Heaven arrayed her. Her our master bought, with the intention of making her recant and marrying her. But she said to him, '*Señor*, it is vain you weary yourself to persuade me to do this thing, for never will I deny my God and His laws, though to lay down my life I am ready.'

"When the master heard this he was wroth, and taking her by the shoulders let her down into a *mazmorra** under his house, binding her with a heavy chain, and feeding her day by day with but six ounces of coarse bread and half a pint of water."

Hearing that, I said I would buy the maid, and redeem her; but they answered it was vain. The Turk would not part with her to any one, and in mockery he had set her price at a hundred millions. So I saw I must have recourse to stratagem, and asked accordingly whether the maid had declared herself a Christian, and they answered, "No, she had only spoken of her God and of His law," then, while I bethought me how to arrange my plan, they exclaimed suddenly, "Here comes

---

* A word borrowed from the Turkish, to signify a dungeon, and used when speaking of a Turkish prison.

the master;" and the moment that he entered the house, eagerly prostrating themselves at his feet, they said:

"Great lord of this mighty *alcázar*,* behold a man who comes to pay the debt of the dead Christian, and who is also desirous to buy the maiden, the slave."

Nor was I sorry to find myself thus launched into the middle of the business, but I stood perplexed, praying in my own mind that God would give me some well-conceived idea which should serve for the redemption of the maiden.

Meantime, I counted out the sum that was due from the dead man; and then I said, "Know you that this Mustafa, my sister, whom you keep in your *mazmorra*,

* Moorish palace.

feeding her with the bread of affliction, is the most pious Jewess of our nation, and that in this you do a great wrong?"

I could proceed no further, for the Moors think it a terrible discredit to have any Jew within their precincts; and this one flew into an ungovernable rage at the bare idea that he had been harboring one; plucking out his beard by handfuls, he cried out with a loud voice of desolation,—

"Woe is me, for my fame and my honor before my people are gone, now that I have suffered this scum of the earth to be with me! Let her be thrust forth from my gates."

So his servants ran and took her up, more dead than alive, and putting her into my arms drove us forth with ignominy and imprecations.

I was no sooner in the street, than I gave great thanks to God for the rescue He had provided, and then I bore her along to the church, thinking she needed the rites of sepulture; but I had scarcely entered the sacred place, than she opened her eyes and breathed. So I gave her such means of refreshment as I had about me, and by degrees the sad lady came to herself; and to give her greater consolation, I bid her observe she was no longer in the estate of a slave, but that by the mercy of Heaven she was redeemed and free.

As soon as her strength had begun to return, I deemed it prudent to run no risk of danger from the Turk, and therefore used every possible diligence to conduct her to the harbor, where at once we went down into my good ship, and giving the crew word to get to sea with all despatch, we were soon steering swiftly between two azure fields.

Thus we came to Venice, my country, where I found that during my absence my dear old father had died; and I should well-nigh have died of sorrow too, but that I had the charge of the beautiful captive lady upon me, and I had to provide for her welfare.

One day I took her aside, and asked her respectfully to tell me what country she was of, and who were her people; but she shook her head in a melancholy way, and bid me ask her nothing, but that with time I should learn all her eventful history. For she came from a far country, and she was not bold enough to propose to me the travail and peril of bearing her home.

"But," I replied, "most beauteous Diana, I asked the question that in the end I might have become thy beloved husband, and if I am not worthy to know thy country, what shall become of my hope?"

And she — "From this day I will be thy beloved wife, for it is thus meet that love should be paid with love."

When I heard this answer, I was beside myself with joy, and instantly arranged everything for the marriage festival, which was celebrated with great pomp and rejoicing, *cañas** and *alcancías*,† music, jousts, and dancing. Among the people who collected from all parts to enjoy the sports, was the captain of one of the ships in port, and he fastened himself on to me with every exterior token of friendship: I too was taken with him, and we were soon inseparable. Nothing would satisfy him, but that one fair bright morning, when our fêtes were over, we should come down to this vessel, that he might give us a banquet there.

* A Spanish game, forming a sort of mock tournament, the combatants being armed with canes instead of lances.

† A Spanish game, consisting in pelting each other with *alcancías*, or round earthen pots, in which flowers and other things were enclosed before they were baked (in the sun), and which fell out when broken against the shield of those at whom they were thrown. I do not know if these games were also in use in Venice, or if their introduction here is a vulgar error.

After this there was dancing, and singing, and much merry-making; and while we were enchanted with the dulcet tones of the marvellous instruments his minstrels played, we failed to perceive we were being carried out to sea.

It was about six in the evening when my beloved bride came and took me by the hand, and said, "Without doubt there is some perfidy, for my heart is filled with fear, and my soul is troubled."

So I took her hand, thinking to reassure her by taking her on shore. But when we came upon the deck, there was nothing to be seen all around but sea and sky, and sea and sky.

My bride, when she saw that, fell into my arms in a swoon; and the cruel captain and half a dozen of his men urged by his command, fell upon me, and tore her from me, and cast me into the sea.

"O Holy Virgin of Carmel," I cried, "and thou S. Anthony of Padua, and Santa Barbara the glorious, and thou my guardian angel, pray for me now, that I perish not in this dire distress!"

As I uttered this petition, I felt a plank of wood strike against my breast; and on it I skimmed the waters all night, and by the first streak of dawn merciful Heaven commanded the waves to throw me upon a soft sandy shore. I could not refrain from kissing the ground which brought me safety; and as I rose up again, I beheld a holy hermit coming toward me, who led me to a little hut, where every day he brought me a basket of sufficient food.

At the end of six months, the hermit came to me very early one morning, and bade me go stand upon the shore, for there a vessel awaited me in which my passage-money was paid.

At the shore I found the vessel, and embarked as the hermit had directed me, not knowing whither we were bound.

At last, after six months' sailing, we came opposite the coast of Ireland, and as we drew near shore, "Friends," said the captain, "it is necessary that this letter and this folded paper be taken to the illustrious King of Ireland; which of you will undertake the charge?"

The crew answered, "*Señor*, let the Venetian take them."

And I, having no aim before me, cheerfully undertook the commission; and springing on shore, went straight to the royal palace, where I found myself in presence of Cæsar's majesty, into whose august hands I delivered the folded paper.

This having opened, he read aloud these words: — "Illustrious Lord! most powerful King of Ireland, the bearer of this letter is a physician of great renown; the sickness of thy daughter, which none can cure, shall flee away at the very sight of him."

Then I was troubled, and would have explained to the King how I was no physician, and the way in which the lot had fallen upon me to bring the letter, which might equally have fallen on the most ignorant sea-boy aboard; and in truth I knew no more of medicaments than the lowest sea-boy of them all.

But the King was overjoyed at the prospect of the healing of his daughter and would listen to no explanations. And in proportion as he manifested his joy, my dismay increased, for I feared his anger when the undeception came.

Meantime, at his command, I was ushered into a vast hall, where were assembled a thousand lords. But, gentle reader, you will well believe me, it was not upon one of them I looked, for at first entering my eye lighted upon a casket covered with emeralds and brilliants which I had given to my beloved bride on the day of our espousals.

I threw myself upon it, crying, "Beautiful Isabella! Ah! where art thou? Where art thou mourning over my grief, as I mourn over thine?"

She, who lay sunk down in the depths of her white couch, at hearing these words darted up from it, and flinging her arms round me, embraced me.

I knew her as our lips met; and full of a thousand joys, we sat talking over the past, forgetful of all present.

And first, I asked what had become of the wicked captain.

"Oh, he!" she said, "when I told my father what he had done, he sent and had him put to death.

"And now," she continued, "did I not tell you that time would reveal to you all about my history? For now that you have seen who and where I am, there is little left to tell. While I was yet little more than a child, my father would have married me against my inclination to a prince of Scotland; and I, knowing his intention, went out from the palace in the night, disguised, upon a swift mare, and when I had ridden a long way, I came to the sea-coast. I found a ship, into which, thoughtless child, I sought refuge, only caring to get away from the prince of Scotland.

"But they were corsairs who manned the vessel; and they carried me off with them to Tunis, where you found me, and set me free from that terrible suffering."

While we were talking, the king came up; and as I was yet musing on the marvellous direction of Providence, by which the lot had fallen on me, rather than another, to come on the embassage to the palace, without which I had been likely never again to have met my bride, it fell into my mind that I had yet the letter to give to his Majesty, which having reached to him, he read thus aloud:

"That I rest in holy ground, my soul at peace, is due to thee; therefore, when the perfidious captain threw thee into the deep sea, I was there; I provided the plank which carried thee to shore; I was the hermit that received and nourished thee;

I was captain of the ship that brought thee to Ireland. And now live long with thy good spouse, and rest after many misfortunes, even as I rest in the eternal habitations."

Then I knew that it was the soul of him I buried at Tunis that had thus befriended me.

Not very long after this the king died, and all the people acclaimed me as their sovereign, where I have been reigning ever since, full of happiness and glory.

EL CLAVEL.*

THE carnation is the flower of predilection of the Andalusian peasant. His cottage does not seem like home without its scent; nor is the maiden's toilet complete without one of its glorious blossoms placed behind her ear, in the ebon setting of her massive hair-braids: it is the token of gladness in their festivals; of love, where coyly offered with a trembling hand. The people sing of its perfections and its meaning in a thousand little ditties.

* The Carnation.

El Clavel.

> Among all the trees of the wood
> The laurel bears questionless sway.
> What maid can compete with my Anna?
> What flower, with carnations, I pray?*

They always speak of it thus, as only next in order to female beauty, and the amorous swain is continually raising the comparison.

> To January's biting frost
> No carnation trusts its charms,
> The tints that Heav'n thy cheeks has given,
> Are dyed ingrain and fear no harms,†

he sings; or perhaps,—

> * Entre los árboles todos
> se señorea el laurel
> entre las mujeres, Ana
> entre los flores, el clavel.

> † En énero no hay claveles
> porque los marchita el hielo
> en tu cara los hay siempre
> porque lo permite el cielo.

El Clavel.

My carnation was raising a plaint,
I ask'd it to tell me its grief,
And it said that thy lips were so fair,
Of their charms it would e'en be the thief.*

The one his fair has given him he declares binds him to her for ever.

The carnation which thou gav'st me,
On holy Thursday last,
Was no flower, but a fetter
To bind me to thee fast.†

The one she nurtures he watches as a token of all that is dearest and most beautiful in her.

* El encarnado clavel
viene publicando agravios
porque no le han hecho á el
hermoso como tus labios.

† El clavel que tu mi diste
el dia de la Ascension
no fué clavel, sino clavo
que clavó mi corazon.

El Clavel.

    My maid has a fav'rite carnation
      Which she watches both early and late;
    I give it a kiss on its petals,
      Whenever I pass by her gate.*

And she in her turn guards her charge with a jealous eye.

    A ruddy carnation have I,
      But I keep it secure from the cold,
    And I shade off the gaze of the sun,
      Lest it tarnish, if he were too bold.†

Such a carnation was once thus tended by a poor village girl: it had grown up, and blossomed, and put forth its deep, rich

---

* En una teja de su casa
   crió mi niño un clavel
   y quando á su vera pasa
   le da un besito en la sien.

† Tengo un clavel encarnado
   á la sombra y bajo llave
   para que el sol no lo vea
   y con mirarlo lo aje.

hues under her care, though she was so poor that she had nothing to grow it in but a broken *olla*.* Nevertheless, when she thought of the happy day when it should become a love-token to one worthy of her, she took such care of it, covering it up when the sun was too hot, watering it with water from the purest spring, sheltering it from the wind, bringing it into her room to guard through the night, lest any evil should befall it, that never carnation flourished so gloriously; it was her only flower, the object of her whole care.

One day there came into the garden a *maja*† in her gala costume. According to

* Pipkin.

† A name employed in Andalusia to designate a person who wears the national costume with great ostentation of correctness, and is altogether what we should term showy.

the pretty Andalusian custom, she carried a bunch of bright, sparkling flowers twisted into her raven hair behind her left ear.

"Ah!" cried the handsome carnation from the depths of its broken *olla*, "why should it not be my lot to adorn the head of this lovely creature, instead of being abandoned to the care of a penniless peasant?"

The *maja* smiled, and passed round the garden two or three times, to see if the carnation persisted in his idea. Every time her black veil caught, as she passed, in the sharp edge of the broken pipkin, the carnation wafted a soft sigh,—

"Ah, why was I not born to adorn that shining hair?"

The *maja* deferred no longer to fulfil his wish: throwing the bunch of showy flowers on to the ground, she plucked the carnation and plaited it into her hair.

Right proud was the carnation to find himself thus grandly enthroned; far too proud to have a thought of compassion for the other flowers cast away for his sake; too triumphant even to smart under the puncture of the hair-pin which fixed him on the *maja's* head. Many a scornful glance he cast at the broken *olla* which had been his nursery, and the cot of the lowly child who had nurtured him.

Thus he was borne about, displaying his beautiful hues in the sun, and charming every one with his perfume all day. Then

night came: the *maja* stood at her *reja*,*
looking out for her serenader. He came
at last, and brought in his hand a beautiful
white rose; the *maja* stretched out her
hand to receive it with delight; with loud
and joyous thanks she placed it on her
head, flinging the hapless carnation from
her without a thought.

Instead of blooming on his lordly stalk
as at the first, the pride and pet of the
peasant maid, he was soon trampled to
atoms by a drove of pigs, passing on their
way to market!

* Ornamented iron-work in front of the lower windows of Spanish houses.

THE ILL-TEMPERED PRINCESS.

THERE was once a poor young knight, and he went out into the world to seek adventures and do knightly deeds. As he went, he met a man standing in front of a long narrow tunnel in a rock, and blowing through it with his cheeks stretched like two ripe pomegranates, to whom the knight called out, "Halloa! fellow, what do you do there?"

And the man made reply, "Disturb me not, your worship, for with my breath I am turning five hundred and thirty-two mills."

The Ill-tempered Princess.

So the knight asked, "Then who are you?"

And the man made answer, "I am Blowo, son of Blowon,* the good blower."

Then the knight said, "Will you come out with me to seek fortune?"

And the man made answer, "Your worship is not readier to ask than I to accept, for I am tired enough of blowing." So he gave one more good strong blow, enough to set the mills twirling for a long time, and walked on behind the knight.

A little farther along they came upon a man toiling up the hill-side, with a load of a hundred and thirty-two hundred-weight upon his back.

To whom the knight called out, "Halloa!

---

* *On* is the Spanish augmentative.

man, you carry more than a wagon with two yoke of oxen! Who are you?"

And the man made answer, "I am Porto, son of Porton, the strong porter."

Then the knight said, "Will you come out with me to seek fortune?"

And the man made answer, "Your worship is not more ready to ask than I to accept, for I am weary of this burden." So he laid the weight down by the roadside, and walked along behind the knight.

A little farther on they came to a long stretch where the road was very straight, and by the side a man walked up and down twisting a rope, to whom the knight cried out, "Halloa! fellow, what do you there? and who are you?"

And the man made answer, "I am Ropo,

son of Ropon, the cunning rope-maker, and I make ropes which none can break."

Then the knight said, "Will you come out with me to seek fortune?"

And the man made answer, "Your worship is not more ready to ask than I to accept, for I am weary of twisting this rope." So he left there his rope by the road-side, and walked along behind the knight.

A little farther on they came upon a man crouched down by the way-side. To whom the knight called out, "Halloa! fellow, what do you there? and who are you?"

And the man made answer, "I am Listeno, son of Listenon, the ready listener."

So the knight said, "What are you listening for?"

And the man made answer, "Blowo has left off turning the mills, and I am listening for the wind to come down from the mountains of Burgos."

"Fellow! the mountains of Burgos are a hundred leagues off."

"What does that signify, if my hearing reaches as far?"

Then the knight said, "Will you come along with me and seek fortune?"

And the man made answer, "Your worship is not more ready to ask than I to accept, for I am weary of straining my ears." So he set up three flags, that all the country might know the wind would be there in three days, and walked along behind the knight.

Then, after three days' journey, they

came in sight of a magnificent castle, extending half a mile every way over the top of a mountain, but all desolate and in ruins; and the way up to it was overgrown with interlacing brambles and briars, so that they could hardly pass through. Then, to increase their difficulty, a heavy storm came on, which would soon have wetted them through; but Blowo cried out,—

"Never fear, your worship; for I will soon clear the air."

So he blew a mighty blast, and sent all the big thunder-clouds travelling back to the Sierra; and they went on toiling up the brake.

When they came up to the castle, they found there was no door or opening, nor any way in. Porto, Ropo, Listeno, and

Blowo wanted to give up the attempt, and pass on farther; but the knight would not hear of abandoning the adventure.

"If your worship is so determined," said Porto, "I'll open a way for you."

So he broke off a huge piece of rock as big as two men, and, standing a hundred yards off, he flung it against the wall, with a noise that could be heard a hundred miles off. The wall trembled and clattered; but it was held together by a stronger than human power, and all Porto's great strength could produce no effect on it.

"Let us go away from here, Master," pleaded Ropo, "this is no place for us. There is something wrong about this place; and the blessing of God is not here."

"No," replied the knight, "we will first learn all about it; there may be work for us."

So they continued walking round the walls to see where they might effect an entrance, and all to no purpose. By and by Listeno exclaimed, "I hear some one cry;" and they all listened, but could hear nothing. So Listeno made them follow him in the direction whence the sound proceeded, till at last they were near enough for the others to hear the sound also; and they went on following it up, till they came to the mouth of a great well all grown over with climbing-plants; when they had cleared these away, the hole looked so black and deep, it seemed as if it went down to the centre of the earth, and up the shaft there came sounds of a woman's wailing, so loud and pitiful, they were all moved to pity, and anxious to run to the relief of the distressed person; but there was no means of telling how to reach the bottom. Then Ropo came forward, and said, "We will all go abroad, and gather five thousand bundles of *esparto* and *palmito** grass, and all five shall set to work to make a long rope; and with that we will reach the bottom."

So said, so done. They gathered five thousand bundles of *esparto* and *palmito* grass, and they all five set to work under Ropo's directions, and twisted away at the rope; and now and then they tied a frag-

* A tall fibrous plant, which covers whole plains in the south of Spain, so called because its spreading leaves give it a certain resemblance to dwarf-palms.

ment of rock to the end and let it down, to see if it reached the bottom. They went on thus for five years, and at last it splashed the water, and when they let it down again it sounded on the rock, and they found only a few feet of the rope was wet, for the water was not deep.

Then Listeno put his ear to the top and told them it was not standing water, but that a brook ran through, along the bottom of the cave. As they were twisting the rope, they talked away about the great deeds each would do; and each had a conjecture as to what they might find at the bottom of the well. They all thought they should find a treasure, and Porto said he would take it up on his shoulders and carry it home for them, though it should weigh as much as all the lead of the Sierra Almagrera.*

But when the rope was finished, and it was a question of who should go down, not one of the knight's followers, though they had been boasting so loudly before, would venture down into the well. So the knight laughed, and said *he* was not afraid; and one end of the rope having been lashed tightly to a rock, the four followers undertook to pay it out steadily, and down the knight descended into the black, gloomy depth.

Day and night he went on steadily descending for three days and three nights,

---

* The Sierra Almagrera is near Carthagena. The mine whose riches have been thus celebrated in a popular tale for many a century, is just now being vigorously worked by an Anglo-French company.

and at the end he came into the water. It was not more than breast-high, so he waded through it for several yards, till he came to a place where the bank widened sufficiently for him to get out and walk along it; and then he came to some trees, and through the trees was an open space lighted by a lurid light which came from a deeper cave. On a sloping bank, covered with shining grass and strange flowers, lay a beautiful princess, all dressed in white and decked with shining jewels; and as she lay, she moaned and cried and prayed for deliverance. So the knight was hastening toward her, and drew his sword to cut the bonds which confined her, but at that instant up started a fierce demon, whom he had not observed before, as he lay coiled up at the mouth of the cave.

"Not so fast, fine *caballero!*" he cried, "for she is mine, and you will have to fight me before you can touch her." The knight disregarded the menace, and continued his way toward the princess, but the air was stiff all around him — though he could see no hindrance, he found he could not make any way toward her.

"Ha! ha!" roared the demon, "my fine *caballero*, you 'll find you will have to do with me at last!"

"And who are you?" shouted the baffled knight; "and what is this beautiful princess to you?"

"I am bound to answer the knight who asks that question," answered the demon, "or it is little you would have learnt from me. Know, then, that this princess was the only daughter of King Euric, to whom belonged all the country as far as eye can see; and she would have succeeded to his kingdom, but her temper was so violent no one could bear with her. Upon the least contradiction she would order a subject to be executed, and her arbitrary conduct was continually involving the kingdom in discontent and trouble. Her father, who tenderly loved her, used to coax her and use every endeavor to soften her, but with no avail. At last, one day she provoked him so sore that in his anger he exclaimed, 'Go to the horned one!' When I heard myself called, I hastened to seize her; but, notwithstanding all my speed, before I could arrive he had revoked the curse, and so I was tricked out of her. This happened several times, but each time fatherly fondness was quicker than my utmost haste. At last a day came when she excited him greatly, and he said again, 'Go to the horned one!' and before he could recall the words that time, he had fallen down a lifeless corpse. So now she is mine, and mine she must remain till some knight will win her in arms from me, and marry her, and restore her to her castle and her kingdom."

"That will I!" said the knight, stoutly; for though he feared the lady's violent temper after what he had heard, his devotion to chivalry bound him to use his best endeavors to deliver her.

Accordingly he drew his sword, and called to the demon to come on. "Remember one thing," said the demon; "if you should win her, she is yours forever; *I* take her back no more."

Meantime, Listeno, at the top of the well, had been reporting to his companions all that he heard going on below, and their curiosity getting the better of their fears, they let themselves down by the rope, and all four arrived in time to witness the terrible contest.

Never was such a fight seen in this world as that between this knight and the demon, and at last the knight cut off the demon's ear. No tongue could describe the demon's rage at finding his ear in the possession of a mortal.

"Give me my ear!" he cried, in tones so sharp that they almost stunned Listeno's sensitive hearing powers.

"Never!" replied the knight, "or, at least, not without a heavy ransom. In the first place, I exact that without further ado you reinstate the Princess in her castle and all her power." The demon stamped and raged, but the knight was firm. The demon was ashamed to go home without his ear, so he thought it best to comply.

The Princess was restored to her throne, the castle was restored to its strength, the garrison was restored to the ramparts, the servants were restored to the halls. The knight married the Princess; great rejoicings and festivities were celebrated,

The Ill-tempered Princess.

and to his four followers were given places of trust and consequence in the palace.

The demon often came to beg for his ear; but the knight felt that at some time or other he might have need of him, so he would not lose his hold over him.

For a time all went well enough, but by little and little the Princess forgot her years of adversity and the debt she owed the knight: she grew more and more wilful, and before a year was out she had become so violent again, that he grew weary of his life, and declared he could no longer endure the continual turmoil. Remonstrance and coaxing were alike unheeded, and it was vain that he tried her father's remedy, for the demon had sworn never to take her back.

In this strait Porto reminded him of the ear he held in hostage, adding, "I will take it upon myself to deliver you of her." So putting the bottle of brine in which the ear was kept into his pocket, he swung the Princess over his shoulder, and all her struggling was useless against "the son of the strong porter."

Thus laden he went to find out the demon. "You are to take back this Princess; she is only fit for your company," he said, when he had found him.

"Not I!" answered the demon, grinning: "I told your master when he *would* have her he must take her for good and all."

"Do you know this ear?" then asked Porto, showing him the bottle.

The demon clutched at it.

"Not so fast!" cried Porto. "If you want to have it back, this is my master's condition: you must take back the Princess along with it."

So, crestfallen, and glad to get his ear back on any condition, the demon accepted the bargain as it was dictated to him; and the Princess, who could not command her temper, never found another knight to deliver her.

TURIAN AND FLORETA.

THERE lived once, in very ancient times, in Spain a young prince, the Infante Turian. He was a very beautiful youth, and the only child of his parents, King Canamor and his consort Leonela: they were thus tempted to indulge him very much, and, as we should say, to spoil him; in fact, he was allowed to have everything he asked for, and when any present or novel article of merchandise was brought to the palace, if it happened to take his fancy, he got into a way of expecting to have it for his own, and no one thought of thwarting him.

One day there came a foreign merchant to the court, who, instead of having a train of mules heavily laden with varieties of his wares to suit all tastes and fancies, was quite alone and unattended, and himself bore his whole stock. It consisted, indeed, of but one little parcel, easily stowed away in the folds of his cloak. The servants were scandalized at such a mean apparatus, and would have driven him away without letting him have a chance of addressing himself to their masters, telling him if he had nothing more to show than the contents of one little case, it was not worth while to trouble them. It was in vain the merchant urged that what he had to show was of priceless value, and in itself alone was worth all the mule-loads of other merchants put together: they held it for idle raving, and bid him begone.

It happened, however, that the Infante Turian was coming home at the moment, and hearing the altercation, his curiosity was piqued to know what it could be that could be counted so precious. He had horses, and arms, and trappings, and gay clothes, and games, and baubles of every sort, and he had wearied of them all. He had acquired them without labor, and he consequently held them without esteem. Now there appeared a chance of some quite fresh sensation; moreover, the merchant himself had a strange air which fascinated him; again, his accent was different from any he had heard before, and suggested that he brought the productions of some climate which had not yet laid its stores at his feet. Proud, too, to show his power in setting the man free from the importunate scorn of the servants, he ordered them to stand back, and then gave the strange merchant permission to open his store.

Assuming an air of mystery, which excited the young prince still more, the merchant, however, now told him he must take him to some private recess apart, as what he had to show must be seen only by royal eyes. The prince accepted all conditions in his eagerness, and was, indeed, rather flattered by this one. As soon as they were quite alone, the strange merchant placed before him a portrait. Yes, nothing but a portrait in a very simple frame! But it was *such* a portrait that it quite turned poor Turian's head. He had never before dreamt of anything so beautiful; he went into ecstasies at first sight, kissed it, gazed at it, paced up and down the hall with it, raved about it, and grew almost frantic, when the strange merchant at last went up to him and said it was time for him to go home, and he must have the portrait to pack up again.

"Pack up again!" cried the prince: "why, I buy it of you at triple, tenfold, an hundredfold its weight in gold!"

The merchant assured him it could not be sold; he required, indeed, a considerable price for suffering it to be seen, but part with it he could not, on any conditions whatever.

The prince threw his purse to him, and ordered him in no measured terms to depart while the way was clear, otherwise he would set on him the myrmidons from whom he had but now released him.

The strange merchant quietly picked up the purse, counted out conscientiously the sum he had named as the price for the sight of the picture, and laid down the rest, deliberately stowed away his fee in his belt, and at the same time took from it, unperceived by the prince, a little box of powder; then suddenly turning round, he scattered its contents over his face, producing instant insensibility. Prepared for the effect, he caught him in his arms, and laid him gently on a bench, and then, possessing himself of his picture, he stealthily left the castle, unperceived by all.

When the Infante Turian came to himself, some hours afterward, of course pursuit was vain; nor could any trace be learnt of the way the stranger had taken.

The prince was furious that, at least, he had not learnt some clue as to the original of the portrait, but there had not been time for a word of inquiry. And when he set himself to recall every detail, all that would come back to his mind was, that on the blue embroidery of the white drapery which veiled the matchless form, he had made out in curious characters the name FLORETA. Armed with this only guide, he determined to roam the world till he discovered the real beauty whose ideal had so absorbed him.

King Canamor and Queen Leonela were inconsolable at the idea of their only son leaving them on so wild an errand; but they had never taught him obedience and self-control, and they could not move him now. All their persuasions could obtain was his consent to be accompanied by the *Conde* Dirlos, an ancient counsellor of great wisdom and authority in the kingdom, who would know how to procure him assistance by land and sea, in whatever enterprise he might be minded to take in hand. But it was stipulated that he was to control him in nothing: simply watch over him, and further his designs, so as to save him from fatigue and danger.

On they wandered for a year and a day, meeting many adventures, and incurring many perils; but no one knew the name of Florèta. Wherever they went it was still a foreign name. At last — it was just the day year that the strange merchant had brought the portrait—their travels brought them to a steep mountain-path, which led down to the sea. At a turn of the winding road, just below them, a tall figure appeared, wrapped in a long cloak, and wearing a high-peaked cap. The prince gave a bound of joy, and shouted to the figure to halt. It paid no heed, however. "Stop! or you are dead!" shouted the prince, at the same time pointing an arrow with unerring aim at a spot a little in advance of the moving figure. As if conscious of what was going on, though he never moved his head, the strange merchant — for it was he, and the prince had instantly recognized him — stood still for an instant, as the bolt rattled in the ground on which he would have stood had he pursued his way three steps further, and then passed on unheeding. The prince shouted more madly than before; but to no purpose; and in another moment the wind of the road had taken him out of sight.

Madly the prince spurred his horse in pursuit, and reached the turn; but no living form was to be seen. The rocks now resounded with the cries and imprecations with which he adjured the magician

— for such he now rightly deemed him — to stand forth. At last, when he was silent from sheer exhaustion, a low but commanding voice from the depths of a neighboring cave bade him listen, but, as he valued his life, advance not.

"Speak!" cried the prince; "nor torture me with longer suspense. What must I do to find Floreta? I am prepared to go to the end of the world, to undergo any hardship, any torture, to find her; but find her I am determined: if you refuse your help, then by help of some other; so you see it is idle to turn a deaf ear."

"By none other help but mine," answered the magician, "*can* you find Floreta; so your threats are vain. But if I had not meant you to see her, I should not have shown you the portrait at first, for I knew its influence could not be other than that it has exercised. I am going to instruct you how to reach her; but first you must give me my guerdon."

"Name it; ask what you will," interposed the impetuous prince; "ask my kingdom if you like; but keep me not in suspense."

"I only ask what is reasonable," answered the magician; "the real is worth a thousandfold the representation;" and he named a price equivalent to a thousand times the sum he had originally received.

Without so much as waiting to reply, Turian turned to *Conde* Dirlos and told him now was the time to fulfil his father's behest by accomplishing this requirement, and begged him to raise the money without an instant's loss of time.

The count remonstrated in vain, and in vain represented the miseries he would be inflicting on the people by requiring, in so sudden a manner, the levy of so large a sum. Turian, blinded by his passion, bid him save his words, as nothing could change his purpose; and the king's orders to obey him having been unconditional, *Conde* Dirlos set out with a heavy heart to comply.

Ten days of anxious suspense during his absence were spent by the prince in wandering over the rugged declivities of the coast: the ardor of his excitement demanded to be fed with deeds of daring and danger. When he was not so occupied, he was seated panting on the topmost crags, scouring the whole country with his eager glance to descry the first impression of the return of the count, with the means of pursuing his desperate resolve.

The day came at last. And afar off, first only like so many black specks, but gradually revealing themselves as *Conde* Dirlos on his faithful steed, and a long file of heavily-laden mules, came the anxiously expected train. And now he never left his point of observation; but cursed the sluggish hours, as he watched the team now steering over the sandy plain, which seemed interminable in expanse, unmeasured by landmarks; now toiling backwards and forwards up the zig-zagged steep, with provoking seeming of being further off one hour than the last, as at each wind they turned upon their steps; now detached liked spectres against the sky, as they crossed from one reach of the lofty sierra to the next.

All things have an end, even Turian's anxious suspense; and as the count at last neared the magician's cave, he descended at break-neck pace to meet him.

"There is the price," said the count, in sad and solemn accents; "but before rendering it out of your hands, stop and consider it;" and as he spoke he removed from the treasure the brilliant red and yellow cloths, the royal colors of Spain, with which it was covered. "Here, from each province of your father's dominions, is the due proportion of the tribute you have demanded. See — will you spend it so?"

The prince darted forward to glance at the goodly sight of so much gold, but drew back with horror.

What could he have seen to turn his flushed cheeks so deadly pale?

"Count!" he cried, choking with fury, "what have you brought to mock me? This is not coin. You have brought me tears, burning tears, instead of gold."

"It is all the same," replied the count; "I saw you were infatuated, and I brought the money in this form, that the sight might warn you of what you are doing, and by its sad horror arrest you. There is time to return it back into the bosom of those from whom it has been wrung, and no harm will have been done. But if you persist you will find the magician will take them for current coin."

"Quite so!" chimed in the voice from the cave; "it is the money I like best. But I cannot stand dallying thus: if the treasure be not handed over at once, the bargain is at an end, and you never hear of me again."

It only wanted this to quench any little spark of pity and misgiving which the old count's judicious stratagem might have awakened. So without further loss of time the prince called to the magician to come forth and take the spoil.

He was not slow to comply, and taking a handful of the weird currency out of each mule-load, rang it on the rock, where it sounded like the clanking of a captive's chains.

"That is good," he said, in a satisfied tone, when he had concluded his scrutiny. "Now for my part of the bargain. I am not of those who fail because I am paid beforehand: you will find me as good as my word, and even better; for I will supply an item of the bargain which you, impetuous youth, never thought to stipulate for, though the most important of all. I will not only instruct you how to see Floreta, I will give you, moreover, the means whereby, if she pleases you, you can take her captive and bear her away."

"Nay, interrupt me not," he continued, as Turian, nettled at the exposure of his want of diplomacy, was about to declare that he had never thought of any other means to captivate her being required but his own smile and his own strong arm; "I must begin, and have but time to complete my directions. You see yon castle on a rock out at sea;" and as his long bony finger pointed westward, there seemed to be traced against the sky the form of a royal castle at about three days' journey, which Turian, who had for ten days been beating about the coast, could have sworn was not to be seen there before. Nevertheless, fascinated by the magician's commanding manner, he durst say nothing but a murmur of assent.

"Then that is your haven; take ship and steer for it. When you reach the land throw down this token," and he gave into his hand a fine coil of silken chains; "follow its leadings till it take you to Floreta, and if she please you, cast it round her, and she is yours."

As he spoke he disappeared from sight with the mules and their burden.

Turian now once more reminded *Conde Dirlos* of his father's command, and bid him provide him with the swiftest galley on all the coasts of the kingdom, manned with the stoutest rowers, and that with the utmost speed.

If the wise old count shrunk from the former mission, his horror was but the greater at this one. He reminded the prince that when the king had given his consent to the adventure, he had not contemplated any other than a loyal undertaking, such as a noble prince might entertain: he would never have trusted him on one of this nature.

Turian felt the force of the reproach, but lacked the strength of character to command himself. Hurried on by his uncontrolled desire, he bid the old man remember that the command to fulfil his orders was quite unconditional, and there was no limit whatever named.

The count owned this was unfortunately true, and as he could prevail nothing by argument, set himself to remedy the Infante's headstrong wilfulness by making the journey as safe as possible. He not only insisted on having the galley examined as to its seaworthiness by the most experienced shipwrights, and selected the steadiest oarsmen to man the banks, but appointed a consultation of all the astronomers of the kingdom to name the day when they might be sure of safe passage, free from winds. It was pronounced that a storm was just then impending which would last ten days, and after that there would be ten days of fair weather, so that if they allowed ten days for their preparations, they would have time to make the journey and return in all security.

The delay seemed another age to the Infante; nevertheless he was now so near the accomplishment of his object that it passed swiftly enough in the enjoyment of the pleasure of anticipation. The count, too, found some relief to his anxieties in the fact that the storm came on at the predicted moment, giving him great confidence that the halcyon days predicted to succeed might be surely counted on.

They came duly; and a shout of admiration rose from the people on the shore as the gallant vessel moved out over the face of the blue, sunlit waters, which glittered as if showered over with every precious stone at each stroke of the countless oars. And those on board were equally entranced with the gorgeous sight as they seemed to soar along over the soft bosom of the crystal deep; and the noble outline of their native mountains, peak above peak, from the verdant slopes where the cattle browsed lazily, to the wild steeps where even the mountain goats ceased to find a footing, receded, with ever-varying forms of beauty, from their sight.

It was not on *these* that Turian's eye rested. His glance was bent on the castle for which they were making, and his thoughts were bound up in the beauteous treasure within. Such confidence had he in the magician's word, that he had laid his arms aside and held only the silken chain that was to be his guiding line to happiness; and toyed with it, thinking how he would throw it round the prized form of the portrait's original, and how he would gaze on her when she was his.

While he was still wrapt in these thoughts they drew near to the mysterious shore, and every one was occupied in admiring the strength and noble proportions of the castle. But Turian had no thought but for the treasure it contained. Springing lightly on to the land, he lost no time in fulfilling the magician's injunctions; and sure enough the chain uncoiled itself, and, wriggling with a serpent's motion, went straight before him to a gate in the castle wall. It was unlocked, and Turian, pushing it aside, gained entrance to a sumptuous garden, at one end of which was a shady arbor, and in a bank of perfumed roses Floreta herself lay asleep. How his heart beat at the sight! Just as she had seemed in the portrait; just as he had pictured her in his sleeping and waking dreams. Riveted to the spot, he stood contemplating her, as well he might, for her complexion was white as snow, or rather as pure crystal, and tinted as the fresh rose yet on the rose-tree.*

The cautious count, fearful of some ambush, had marshalled the crew of the galley into a guard to track his steps noiselessly, and be ready in case of sudden attack. The play of light upon their arms passing in sudden reflection over the scene woke the Infante from his reverie, and roused him to action. The coiling silken links readily embraced Floreta's limbs, and such was their hidden power that, though she woke at the Infante's

---

* Mirandola está mirando
Que bien era de mirar;
Blanca es como la nieve
Y como lo claro cristal,
Colorada como la rosa
Y como rosa de rosal.

approach, she was powerless to resist or cry.

Thus he bore her to the galley, and the men having resumed their places on the rowers' banks, in silent order they pushed off unperceived by any one on the island, for it was the hour of the noontide rest.

But soon Floreta's maidens, coming to attend her rising, discovered her loss. The king, her father, and all the people quickly gathered their arms and ran wildly in every direction, till at last they saw the strange vessel making fast away, and they doubted not it was carrying off their princess, but they could only stand on the shore throwing up their arms and crying in powerless despair.

Turian had in the meantime removed

the chain from his prize; and thus freed from the spell, Floreta, too, held out her arms toward her parents and countrymen, and cried unavailingly on them for help. Turian, incapable of contradicting her, yet incapable also of giving her up, contented himself with admiring her at a distance, and let her spend herself in lamentations at first; but when the good galleon had put sufficient distance between itself and the castle to destroy the freshness of the impression of parting, the Infante commanded his people to cast anchor, that he might try his power of consoling her more at ease. And, indeed, it was not long before his sweet words of admiration and his protestations of affection and devotion seemed to succeed in reconciling her to her situation; before long they were very good friends and very happy, and the sun shone, and the sea sparkled, and nature smiled, and all seemed fair and bright.

Nevertheless, the prudent old count had his misgivings. True, there were yet several more days of the promised calm before them, but he felt he should never be easy till he had his charge safe at home again; so he urged the Infante to give orders to put under way once more, and right glad was he to feel the bark moving toward the port, and in good time to reach home before the next storm.

Nevertheless,—

> Quando Dios quiere
> En sereno lluve,*

* If God so will, it may rain with a clear sky.

says the proverb, and while they were singing and making merry, and dancing to amuse Floreta, suddenly the sky became overcast, and the wind sprang up, and the waves dashed against the bulwarks, and instead of being able to row the vessel into port, the oarsmen could hardly keep their seats. Then, in the midst of their fright and horror and piteous cries for help, an ancient seaman stood up, and having commanded silence, harangued the crew, and told them that they might be sure the tempest was sent them, because they had the strange damsel on board; that if they would save their lives they must bid defiance to the Infante's wishes, and take him from her and cast her into the sea. The danger to all was manifest and terrible; any way out of it was preferable to succumbing, so the old man found a willing audience. The dismayed count had but time to rush into the Infante and tell him of the mutiny, before the angry mariners had already burst into his presence. If they were for a moment staggered by pity at sight of the exceeding beauty of Floreta, and by Turian's agonized assurances that the fearful sacrifice would have no effect upon the storm, the old mariner's voice overruled their hesitation and rendered them pitiless as the blast.

Then at his command they tore the Infante from off Floreta, to whom he clung, declaring that they should not destroy her without him, but that he would go down into the deep with her, and they bound him fast, hand and foot, and took Floreta, too full of terror to resist or cry, to throw her into the raging sea. But before they had completed the sacrifice, the cries of the prince, seconded as he was by the prudent old count, ever ready to second a middle course, prevailed, and instead of committing her to the deep, they set her on an island past which the bark was drifting, Turian thinking in his own mind that as soon as the fury of the storm was spent he should be able to induce them to put back and fetch her off.

The old seaman knew what was in his mind, and he knew that the work was but half done. He inveighed that the half-measure was useless; he predicted that the storm would not thereby be quenched. But it was too late to listen to him now: they were carried past the land where Floreta was; and it was beyond their efforts to go back to fulfil his purpose now. Meanwhile, as he had predicted, the tempest raged higher and higher; the oarsmen were powerless: but the bark drifted nearer and nearer home; and at last, just as a great wave dashed against it and broke it up, they were brought just so near to land that they could swim to shore. One young and vigorous oarsman took charge of the old count, who was rendered more unfit for the feat by dismay at the ill-success of his mission, even than by the weakness of his age. But none looked after the Infante, for he was known to be the expertest swimmer of all the country round.

It was not till the hull had heeled over and gone down that they remembered they had bound him hand and foot, and he could not escape. And so he, who was the cause of all, alone was lost.

THE PEDRO JIMENEZ GRAPE.

THERE was a well-to-do vine-grower named Pedro Jimenez, who cultivated a small tract of land on which his fathers had lived for many generations before him, and had been known throughout the district for men of undoubted *pundonor*, by which word Spaniards express the most scrupulous nicety of honorable conduct. Blessed with all other worldly advantages, Pedro Jimenez had one great trial — he had no child to whom to transmit the name he had received from his predecessors, and himself borne so creditably. When he reflected on this, there was one thought in the background which used to distress him. There was living at a sufficient distance to be quite unknown to his neighbors, a poor relation of his wife, whom he assisted frequently in secret; but he had never let the knowledge of the humiliating circumstance transpire. Yet he knew that this poor hard-working man with difficulty kept his family above want; that the greatest delicacy in which they could ever indulge was the dish popularly called *duelos y quebrantos* (sorrows and troubles), a stew made up of the poorest odds and ends and leavings,* in bitter mockery of the favorite Spanish *olla*

* There is so little trace of flesh-meat in it that it was allowed on fast-days.

podrida, which is a compound of the most succulent meats and vegetables.

Conscience would whisper in Pedro Jimenez's ear, "Here, in this poor fellow's son, is an heir whom you may adopt; take him from the present temptations to discontent and dishonesty with which privations ply him, and bring him up according to the traditional maxims of your house." But when he thought of the details of bringing the ragged lad to his respectable homestead, and the neighbors pointing to him as the relation of the wealthy Pedro Jimenez, his courage failed him, and he turned from the idea. So years passed by, and this thought remained the weak point of Pedro Jimenez's otherwise irreproachable character.

One evening, as he was strolling through his vineyard, admiring the beautiful clusters of grapes which were his riches for the coming year, he was disturbed by the mournful howling of a dog, proceeding from the road-side at no great distance. His kind heart prompted him immediately to follow up the sound, and he was not long before he came upon a saddening sight. On the ground lay the prostrate form of a delicate youth, foot-sore and travel-worn, and now brought to a state of unconsciousness through exhaustion; by his side there lay a large shaggy dog of pitiable aspect; his bones almost protruded through his skin, his eyes were glassy and wild, and he trembled in every limb. His melancholy howling grew fainter and fainter, and by the time Pedro Jimenez got up to the group, he saw he was past the reach of help; with one more distressful howl, he rolled on his back and expired, having spent his last breath in summoning aid to his young master!

Pedro Jimenez lost no time in raising the youth in his arms, and bearing him to his own comfortable home, where his wife's kindly care soon restored him to animation. Refreshed by her attentions, he was soon able to tell his tale; and what was the surprise of the good couple, when they learnt that the poor child they had so charitably entertained was no other than the son of their poor relation. Nevertheless, his history was a sad one. His father and mother had both fallen victims to an epidemic disorder in their village; kind neighbors had taken in the younger children, a convent had provided for two older girls; and the eldest boy, having been used to labor all his life, had manfully resolved to be a charge to no stranger, but had set out to seek the advice and direction of the only relation he had to look up to, in finding work by which he could support himself, and lay by enough to portion his younger sisters. As the weary boy told his tale of domestic heroism, Pedro Jimenez's better nature stirred within him. He no longer stifled the dictates of conscience, no longer suffered himself to be governed by a false and foolish fear of human respect, but took his young kinsman by the hand, told him he was proud of his spirit, and that as Heaven had denied him direct heirs, he would henceforth make it depend entirely on his own good conduct to become the heir to his comfortable competence.

The orphan lad was overjoyed at the prospect. In his little world the name of Pedro Jimenez had all his life stood as the embodiment of all that was respectable, and desirable, and worthy of imitation. To be suddenly elevated to the position of aspiring to one day himself inheriting that honored name, with all its contingent advantages, was greater happiness than he had ever dared to entertain in his wildest dreams.

Pedro Jimenez had every reason to be satisfied with the decision he had come to.

All the neighbors who were sufficiently men of worth to make their opinion a matter of consequence, far from looking down on him for the disclosure, warmly applauded his generosity; and in return for the few worthless ones whose acquaintance he lost by it, he won for himself the affection of a devoted son. The old man had never known a greater pleasure than that he now found in taking his adopted child out with him day by day, and instructing him in all the various arts of treating the vine — the mode of planting and culture, the vintage, the pressing of the grape, and the disposal of the wine; and to all this, his young charge listened with an earnestness and intelligence that repaid all his care. His frugality, and industry, and straightforward manly conduct on all occasions — his almost feminine kindliness of manner in supplying, to the best of his power, the offices of the old wife, when God took her home, all rendered the old man quite easy as to the future successor to his name.

At last the time came when Pedro Jimenez the elder, full of years and honor, was called to his account; and as his adopted son turned to meet the desolation of the lonely house, there was one thought of consolation to gild his bereavement, the sense that he could make his whole after-life a token of obedience to the upright maxims of his benefactor, in whose stead he now stood.

While our hero had been living in rustic

tranquillity in the remotest part of the south of Spain, great events had been stirring Europe. The tumultuous tide of the French Revolution had overflowed the Peninsula. I will not detain you with anything you can consider a dry epitome of history. Suffice it to say, that in consequence of the troubles in which his country was involved, young Pedro Jimenez was called to join the army.

Having felt, as I hope you have, some interest in the honest pride with which he was on the point of entering on his inheritance, I am sure you will sympathize with the sadness of heart which now overshadowed him as he was obliged to abandon his fair homestead just as it had become his own. "It is well the old man never suspected it would come to this!.. and then peace must come and restore me to my home some time or other," he used to say to comfort himself during the weary march or tedious drill. There was, however, yet a heavier trial in store. It was the policy of the intruded French ruler to send away the native troops out of their country, and replace them with French troops. Now it happened that Pedro Jimenez was attached to the regiment of General Romano, which was one of those selected for foreign service. Ordered to the banks of the Rhine, poor Pedro Jimenez seemed farther than ever from the fulfilment of his darling hopes. He had perhaps felt the defence of his country some compensation for the separation from home; but to fight for the unjust aggressions of one who was the usurper of the throne of his native land was surpassingly hard. When not joining his comrades in lamenting their hard fate, he would wander over the country, trying to find any incident which might remind him of his beloved Andalusia. His attention was thus arrested by the vines which he found growing on the heights around. The knowledge of the subject he had acquired during so many years' apprenticeship, and under so experienced a master, now proved invaluable. His practised eye readily distinguished among the varieties presented to it a superior variety adapted to the soil and climate of Andalusia, and he determined, whenever Providence was pleased to give him an opportunity of returning, that he would provide himself with the means of propagating this stock in his own plantation.

Nor was this opportunity very long withheld. General Romano, though scarcely taller than the length of an ordinary man's arm,* bore in his little body a large and loyal heart: by dint of persevering efforts, he succeeded in making a way of escape for his whole regiment, shipped them, and carried them safely round to a friendly port of Portugal, and thence draughted them all back into Spain, where they did good service under Wellington.

Pedro could hardly believe his ears for joy, when the mysterious order was trans-

* Tamaño como del codo á la mano.

mitted to him, to prepare for the secret return: yet he did not in his transports forget the coveted vine. The plant thus obtained, tended and preserved with much care and anxiety through the voyage, might still have been condemned to perish, had he been called to active service; but the rough life and the long voyage had impaired his health. After several months in hospital, during which time, you may be sure, he did not neglect his precious plant, he was sent home invalided.

He found his own *viña* in a sad state of neglect; but his native air having soon restored his strength, he was able within a few years more, not only to bring it round again, but also to produce a goodly show from his newly imported vine-stock.

And from this vintage it is — the Rhenish stock planted in Andalusian soil, and cultivated with tender care and intelligence — that we get the choice variety of sherry wine (you can ask Papa to let you taste it some day at dessert,) called "Pedro Jimenez."

MOORISH REMNANTS.

I.

ISSY-BEN-ARAN.

THOUGH the Moors were always hated in Spain, first as a conquering, and afterward as a conquered race, yet many poetical traces of their traditions and maxims remain in the popular literature of the country; and in some of these they appear in a very advantageous light, though, of course, the national hatred loved rather to record those of a contrary import.

Issy-ben-Aran was a venerable muleteer, well-known in all the towns of Granada for his worth and integrity — an elder and a father among his tribe.

One day, as he was journeying over a wild and sequestered track of the Sierra Nevada, he heard a cry of pain proceeding from the road-side. The good old man immediately turned back to render help to the unfortunate. He found a young man lying among the sharp points of an aloe hedge, groaning as if at the last gasp.

"What ails thee? Son, speak," said Issy-ben-Aran.

"I was journeying along the road, father, an hour agone, as full of health as you may be, when I was set upon by six robbers, who knocked me off my mule, and not satisfied with carrying off all I possessed in the world, beat me till they thought I was dead, and then flung my body into this aloe hedge."

Issy-ben-Aran gave him a draught of water from his own *bota*,* and bound his head with linen cloths steeped in fresh water; then he set him on his own beast, to carry him at a gentle pace to the nearest town and further care for him, with great strain of his feeble arms lifting him tenderly into the saddle.

No sooner was the stranger well mounted, with his feet firmly set in the stirrups, than, drawing himself up with no further appearance of weakness, he dug

* Small leathern bottle, hung from the saddle in travelling.

his heels into the horse's side, and setting up a loud laugh, started off at a rapid gallop.

Issy-ben-Aran, to whom every stone of the road was known as the lines upon his right hand, immediately scrambled down the mountain-side, so as to confront the stranger at the turning of the road.

"Hold!" he cried. And the nag, who loved his master well, stood still and refused to move for all the stranger's urging.

"Son! think not I am come to reproach you," said the old man. "If you desire the horse, even take it as a gift; you shall not burden your conscience with a theft on my account."

"Thank you!" scoffed the heartless

stranger. "It is fine to make a merit of necessity; but I have nothing to do but ride to the nearest town, and sell the brute."

"Beware! and do it not," said the old man. "The nag of Issy-ben-Aran is known at every market in the kingdom, and any man of all our tribes who frequents them, finding you with him, will reckon you have killed me, and slay you in turn. Even for this have I come to you: take this scroll to show that you have it of me as a free gift, and so no harm shall come to you.

"Only one condition I exact. Bind yourself to me, that you tell no man of what has passed between us; lest peradventure, should it become known, a man hearing his brother cry out in distress, might say, 'This man is feigning, that he may take my horse like the horse of Issy-ben-Aran,' and the man who is really in danger be thus left to perish miserably."

MOORISH REMNANTS.

II.

MÓSTAFA ALVILÁ.

MÓSTAFA ALVILÁ was califf of a conquered province in Spain, where he reigned with oriental state. The tributary people were ground down with hard work to minister to his treasury, and the vast sums he amassed were spent in beautifying his alcázar, and filling it with costly productions from all parts. Merchants from every climate under heaven were encouraged to come and offer him their choicest wares.

One day a merchant of Persia brought a large pack of shawls and carpets, all woven in gold and pearls, and wools and silks of brilliant colors, but among them all the most beautiful was one carpet of great price, on which Móstafa Alvilá's choice was immediately set; but in all his treasury there was not found the price of it. Nothing would do, he *must* possess it: then Ali Baba his vizier came forward and said, "Let ten thousand dogs of Christians be sold, and with the price of them you shall purchase the carpet."

Móstafa Alvilá answered and said, "The advice is good!" So they sent and sold ten thousand Christians, and with the price of them the carpet was bought.

Móstafa Alvilá sat contemplating the curious devices, and tracing the wonderful arabesque patterns with which the carpet was covered; and there was one pattern, all shining with gold and pearls, quite prominent in the centre, which had a likeness to the characters of an inscription; and when Móstafa Alvilá saw it, he was very curious to know if it was an inscription, and what it meant, so he sent to recall the merchant; but he was gone from the alcázar. Then he sent his servants after him, and though they travelled three days' journey by every road, they could neither find him nor obtain any tidings of whither he had passed. Then Móstafa Alvilá was more curious, and sent and gathered all the learned men in his califate, and inquired of them what the inscription might mean. They all looked troubled, and said they could not tell; they had never seen such letters. But one there was who concealed the difficulty he was in so ill, that Móstafa Alvilá saw he knew what the writing meant, so he looked very severely upon him, and threatened him with instant death if he did not tell him exactly what the writing was.

Then the interpreter, when he found there was no other way to save his life, with great fear and trembling said, this is the meaning thereof:

"SHIROES, SON OF CHOSROES, KILLED HIS FATHER; AND HE DIED SIX MONTHS AFTER."

Móstafa Alvilá was greatly troubled when he heard the sentence; for *he* had ascended the califate by killing his father, and he had reigned six months all but one day. So he sent and commanded that the interpreter, and all who had heard the sentence, should be put to death, that no one might know the omen.

But that night, in the middle of the dark hours, when Móstafa Alvilá was alone in his chamber, a horrible vision came to him. He thought he saw the body of his father, whom he had murdered, rise up to convict him. He sunk down in his bed, and covered his face in fear and horror.

In the morning, when they came to call him, they found only his lifeless corpse.

MOORISH REMNANTS.

III.

THE EMIR IN SEARCH OF AN EYE.

THE Emir Abu-Bekir lost an eye in battle against the Christians. "The Christians shall pay me what they have taken from me," he said; and he sent for a number of Christian captives, and had one of their eyes taken out, in the idea of replacing his own; but it was found that none of them agreed with his in size, and form, and color. The Emir Abu-Bekir was of very comely person, and his eyes had been so mild and soft, that it was at last thought only the eye of a woman could replace the missing one; the choice fell upon a beautiful maiden named Sancha. Sancha was brought into the Emir's presence, and his physician was ordered to take out her eye, and place it in the vacant socket.

Now Sancha stood trembling and wailing, and by her very crying damaging the perfection of the coveted feature. Then there stood up a travelling doctor, who was in great fame among the people, and begged a hearing of the Emir; for albeit he was a Turk, yet he possessed pity and gratitude. He knew that the operation, while a torment to the Christian maiden, would be of no service to the Emir; and he pitied the waste of pain. It happened further, that once, when on a journey, he had sunk fainting by the way-side, this very Sancha had comforted and relieved him; and now he determined to rescue her.

Accordingly, he stepped up to the Emir, and told him that he had eyes made of crystal, and colored by cunning art, which no one could tell from living eyes, and which would be of much greater service and ornament than those of the Christian dogs, whose eyes, he might have observed, lost all their lustre and consistency the moment they were taken from their natural place. The Emir admitted the truth of the last statement, and being marvellously pleased with the glass eyes the travelling doctor displayed, asked him the price.

"The maiden for a slave," replied the doctor.

The Emir gladly consented to so advantageous a bargain, and suffered the glass eye to be fixed in his head. All the Court applauded the appearance.

"But I cannot see with it!" cried the Emir.

"Oh! you must give it a little time to get used to your ways," answered the doctor, readily; "you can't expect it all of a sudden to do as well as the other, that you have had in use so long."

So the Emir was content to wait; meantime, the doctor made off with his fair prize, whom he conducted safely back to Spain, and restored her faithfully to her friends and her liberty.

MOORISH REMNANTS.

IV.

YUSSUF'S FRIEND.

THE merchant Yussuf took great pains to train up his only son in prudence, that he might be able, when he was no more, to carry on his business, as he had done before him, with credit and success. But in spite of all his lessons, he would be continually putting his confidence in worthless persons; and in particular he fostered an intimacy with a young Jew of dangerous character, who had several times, by fraud and cunning, cheated him out of large sums, all the while leading young Yussuf to believe that what he had done was fair and just; nor would he listen to his father's suspicion of him.

The merchant Yussuf had to take a journey to Africa with his son; and while preparing for it, he lamented loudly over the difficulty he was in as to placing his money in safety during his absence.

"Now, if you had not been so suspicious of my friend the Jew," said young Yussuf, "*there's* a man who would have taken care of it for you!"

"You know my opinion of him," replied his father.

"Ah! you're so suspicious," replied young Yussuf, "*I* know him better."

"Well, if you think so well of him, I will, on your advice, ask him to take care of a strong-box for me."

"Well done, father!" replied the young man; "you'll see you'll never repent it."

The same evening, the merchant Yussuf sent a large chest, heavy enough to contain a vast amount of treasure, to the Jew, by the hand of his son; and the next day they set out for Africa.

Having brought their affairs to a prosperous termination, the two Yussufs returned home to Granada.

On the morrow of their arrival, the merchant sent his son to the Jew, to reclaim the strong-box. Young Yussuf returned presently, full of indignation.

"Father, you have insulted my friend

beyond all possibility of reconciliation. He tells me it was not money you entrusted to his keeping, but a parcel of broken stones!"

"And pray," replied his father, "how did your honorable friend discover what was in my strong-box? To find this out, he must have broken my locks; which will, I think, show you it was very well I gave no greater value into *his* keeping."

Young Yussuf hung his head, and suffered himself to be guided after that by his father's experience in his judgment of mankind.

MOORISH REMNANTS.

V.

THE SULTANA'S PERFUMER-IN-CHIEF.

OF all the luxurious appointments of the Moorish houses, none were more prominent than the baths. And you must not think that means a bath just big enough to get into, like those in our houses. At Seville and Granada, and wherever the Moors lived and built, you may see remains of the vast constructions which served them for baths, all of white marble, and situated in the midst of scented shrubs and sweet and brilliant flowers.

In their own hotter country, their baths received a still greater development. There was once a sultana, Moorka-Hama, who had a fancy to have *her* baths always filled with rose-water. One day, when she came to bathe, she found the air perfumed to a most unusual degree; and on her causing an inquiry into it, they found that the heat of the sun had expressed the essential oil, which was floating on the surface. The process thus suggested by accident, was immediately imitated by art; and by it is produced the delicious scent which is now an article of commerce, and which we call attar of roses.

ARAUCANIA THE INDOMITABLE.

I.

AMONG the many traditions of Spanish adventures in the West Indies and Americas, none are more interesting than those concerning Araucania. Araucania is a province of Chili, which was inhabited by the bravest and noblest tribe of aborigines. Their courage and patriotism preserved them from ever succumbing to the invaders. When the rule of Spain was at length effected, it was through the conversion of the natives and their voluntary acceptance of a Christian government — never by their subjugation; so much so, that for years it was commonly known by the name of "El Estado indomito" (the unconquered province).

Various stories are told of heroism on both sides which deserve a place beside the noblest and most celebrated deeds of any history. Don Alonso de Ercilla y Zuñiga was a page in attendance on Philip II. at the Court of our Queen Mary, when news came of a fresh outbreak of the indomitable Araucanians. Though a mere lad, he pleaded for permission to join the expedition which was immediately formed to quell the insurrection. He presents a marked instance of the best type of Spanish character — brave and patriotic, and at the same time chivalrous and generous. The intervals of leisure he could snatch from the business of the campaign were spent in recording in an heroic poem (which he wrote on any scraps of paper he could procure, and when these failed, on dried skins of animals,) the incidents of the war which struck his poetic fancy. Far from attributing all the merit to those of his own side with the spirit of a partisan, he has left a series of most touching pictures of the nobleness and bravery of his antagonists. His poem begins, after the manner of the Iliad, with a list of all the valiant chiefs, detailing their qualities, and the numbers they commanded. Then it goes on to give a stirring description of their meeting to excite each other to rise in the defence of their country. There was no hanging back or cowardly fear,—every one was anxious to be foremost to the fray. When they had well eaten, and warmed their courage with deep potations from their *tinajas** of wine, up rose Tucapel the audacious, and declared he was ready to head the expedition. The universe knew he was the bravest of them all; and if any one disputed the boast, he was ready there and then to make it good. Not suffering him to conclude his speech, Elicura broke in full of boldness, "To *me* it is given to lead the affair; and if any one dispute the claim, he must taste the point of my lance."

"To *my* arm! to *my* arm," cried Ongolmo, "it behooves to brandish the iron club."

* Large jars.

"Folly!" shouted Lincoya, mad with rage. "It is mine to be lord of the world, as certainly as my hand holds the oaken staff."

"None surely," interposed Argol, "is so vain as to put his prowess on a par with *mine*."

But Cayocupil, shaking his heavy spear, cleared a free space around him, and roared, "Who will dispute *my* right to be first? Let him come on, come on! I can match you, one or all."

"I accept the challenge!" responded Lemolemo, darting toward him, "it is no effort to me to prove what is already mine of right."

But Puren,* who was drinking at a dis-

---

* Puren distinguished himself so much by his courage in

tance, here dashed furiously through the crowd, and proudly asked who dared harbor so insane a thought; declaring that where Puren stood no one else could bear command. When the storm was at its highest, all shouting and shaking their spears, the venerable Colócolo, the most ancient of all the caciques, came forward, and silence was made before him.

"Caciques, defenders of the State!" he said, "no desire of command animates me; already by my great age I half belong to the other world; my love of you all alone impels me to give you the counsel of the white-haired. But spend not against one another the courage which is needed

---

these wars, that Alvárez de Toledo, a captain in the Spanish army in Araucania, composed a poem on him, entitled, "Puren indomito."

against our common foe; fight not as to which of you is most valiant, for you are all equal in prowess, as in birth and possessions, and any one of you is worthy to govern the world. But as to which shall lead in this present expedition, be advised by me: there must be one, and let the choice be decided by a trial of endurance. Whichever of you shall longest support a baulk of timber of exceeding weight without wearying, *he* shall take the lead."

He spoke, and not one voice was raised against the voice of the ancient. So the baulk of timber was brought—a vast trunk of ebony, which a man could scarcely clasp round with his arms. Paycabi came forward to make the essay, and planted it on his broad shoulders; six hours he bore it with a steady strain, but he could not complete the seventh. Cayocupil with an agile step walked up to the beam, and bore it five hours; Gualemo, a well-grown youth, tried it after him, but could not endure it so long; Argol took it next, but gave way at the sixth hour, and Ongolmo only kept it half an hour more. Puren after him bore it half a day; Lebopia, four hours and a half. Elicura stood up under it manfully longer than any, but at the ninth hour he gave in. Tucápel supported it fourteen hours, and went round to all the caciques boasting of the feat; which, when Lincoya perceived, he tore the cloak from his terrible shoulders, and raising the ponderous bulk without the least apparent strain, planted it on his back, curved ready to receive it. Then he ran hither and thither to show how slight was the effort to him. He took it up at the rising sun, and he bore it till the sun had returned to his rest, and through the dread night Diana kept watch with him; and the sun rose again upon his labors, yet he laid it not down till mid-day. And all the people were astonished to find there was one so powerful among them, and they began already to attribute to him the honors of the generalship.

Then Caupólican came up to take his turn quietly and alone — from his birth one of his eyes had been deprived of light; but what was wanting in his power of vision was made up to him in his surpassing strength.

He was a noble fellow, comely and strong, dignified in his bearing, and made for command, upright and unflinching, and a strict maintainer of that which is right. His form was muscular, lithe and agile, deep-chested and erect. With the ready confidence of assured superiority, he lifted the wood as if it had been a straw, and poised it gracefully on his shoulders. And all the people praised the movement with a shout of admiration; then Lincoya quailed, for he began to fear the victory would be taken from him. But how much more, when the hours passed by and the hero gave no sign of weariness: he paced up and down, conquering fatigue by resistance, and increasing his power by the habit of endurance. Thus through two days and two nights he never flinched, and then, as if because he had done enough—not because he was exhausted, he lifted down the weight and flung it from him to a mighty distance, showing his strength still unimpaired.

Then all the people shouted and said Caupólican was their leader, and the fear of him was so great, that even those at a distance obeyed his word as if he had been present. Caupólican first exerted his command in setting order among his ranks, and assigning a place to each cacique and his followers. Then he made out a sagacious plan of attack on the Spaniards, and stirred up the brave Araucanians to the contest by assuring them of a speedy victory. Some advised this, and some that, but Caupólican, with his serene word of command, reduced all to willing obedience.

The Spaniards had set up three forts to strengthen their hold on the territory, and against the most formidable of these the first attack was directed. The rising being quite unsuspected, the natives approached the fort easily; but when the Spaniards saw the horde approaching, they quickly raised the cry to arms, and sallied out to meet them with supercilious impetuosity. They soon found, however, they had no mean foes to deal with; though weary and footsore with their hasty march, the Araucanians no sooner came in presence of the foe, than they fought with all the pride and confidence of assured victory. Resistance met resistance, for hours neither side wavered, till at last the Spaniards were glad to secure their retreat in good order into the fort.

Now there was in the Spanish army a brave youth, who, seeing his countrymen give way before the barbarians, was moved to indignation; and when the gate of the fort had closed on the last of them, he stood alone * on the drawbridge, and cried to the insurgents, "Come on! come on, the most valiant of you! One at a time, I will match thirty of you — nay, I refuse not to a thousand."

More than a hundred Araucanians ran hotly to the encounter; but undismayed,

---

* It is possible Don Ercilla here celebrates some feat of his own.

that Spanish youth stood boldly on the bridge, and yet he called to them to come on. Firm and erect he met them, and with a well-placed stroke of his trusty sword laid one, and again another, and another, on the ground. His comrades, watching the unequal contest, sallied through a postern of the fort, and made a diversion for his relief. Many such devoted deeds were done on both sides that day; but it was vain the Spaniards fought like lions, for on and on the Araucanians poured, and for every Spaniard they were twenty. Then, when it was useless to resist longer against their overpowering numbers, they agreed during the night-time to abandon the fort; and trusting to the swiftness of their steeds, they rode away to a place of greater safety. So Caupólican and his caciques with great rejoicing took possession of the place, and laid the fort even with the ground.

ARAUCANIA.

II.

TEGUALDA.

IT happened once, after there had been a desperate encounter between the Spaniards and Araucanians, that Don Alonso de Ercilla went out late at night to meditate on the lessons of the battle-field, strewn with the bodies of those who had been well and brave but a few hours before. The night was dark and gloomy, and yet he thought he discerned indistinctly a form moving from place to place, quietly and noiselessly as a spirit might move; and anon there came from it sighs and groans dismal to hear. Bending down, and hiding himself in the long grass, he tracked the figure, not without some fear at heart; but clasping his trusty sword, he came swiftly upon it. Then it rose erect, and addressed him in humble, timorous accents: "Señor, Señor, have pity on me; I am but a woman, and never have I offended you! If my misery does not move you to spare me, at least consider that there is no glory to be gained by killing a woman — or rather, slay me, but first let me fulfil my work." Then Don Ercilla asked her what it was had brought her there. And she in dolorous tones answered, "Never was grief like mine; I loved him with true love and purest constancy, and to-day he was taken from me, and slain. Let me but seek the body of him who was my soul, and let me lay it in a decent grave, and *then* take my life, lay my body beside his, for so great is my grief that I dread living without him more than lying beside him in death."

Don Ercilla was greatly moved by her sorrow, but still he had his duty as a soldier to consider; she might have come to spy the situation of the Spanish camp, under the idea that, as a woman, she would be less easily suspected; and her grief might be assumed in order to induce him to release her. Yet his compassion swayed him at last, so he let her live, and moreover assisted her in her search, leading her to relieve her oppressed heart by pouring out all her story.

"Woe is me!" she said, "for no relief is possible for me, no rest till death. He is gone, and if I open now the old wounds by thinking of him, it is but in the hope that in the violent effort I may sink and die.

"Know then, that I am Tegualda, daughter of the cacique Brancol. Vain of the attentions that were paid me through many young years, I refused to listen to the suits of any of the young caciques whom my father presented to me; nor when they danced or wrestled before me would I regard them with favor.

"One day my father took me to the shady thicket where gentle Gualebo pours its limpid stream into the floods of broad Itata with a soothing murmur, and where the sunlight playing through the thick foliage of the breeze-shaken trees, diapered the perfumed air.

"Scarcely had we sat down, when there entered on the plain that spread away before us a band of youths, earnest and silent. At a sign from Brancol various games began, in which each exerted himself to the utmost only to win a glance from me. To me, however, it was a greater pleasure to stand detached from them all, and while they ran, and fought, and showed strange feats of endurance, rather than gratify them by a look, to rest my eyes on the murmuring stream, watching the polished stones, now bathed in snow-like foam, now piercing, black and stark through the mimic waves; or on the waving trees, flinging their lithesome limbs in every graceful attitude, now wide apart, now interlaced in one another's thrall; or on the far-off sky, sparkling and peering through the leafy shade; on anything rather than on the contending youths; and thus I sat there, disdaining all interest in the games, and, as I deemed, fancy-free, when all at once a loud cry rose from the contending throng: this was no unusual occurrence, but it was so exulting and prolonged that I could not choose, but ask the cause. The youth who stood nearest me made answer, 'Did you not observe, Señora, how the brave Mareguano has won the victory over every other combatant? and now when, with joyous haste, we were leading him to receive the conqueror's wreath from your hand, to gird his temples in token that he is the first and bravest of our company — all at once that handsome lad yonder, wearing green and scarlet for his device, suddenly confronted him, and at their first contest laid him low on the green sward. Mareguano no sooner regained his feet than he required to be allowed another trial; but as this is against all our rules, it was refused him. So the stranger youth comes to be crowned by you, unless you, whose power is absolute over us, suffer them to renew the contest.'

"As he spoke, the shouting crowd led him up to me; but before I could take the wreath to crown him, he placed himself modestly before me on his knees, and thus spoke: —

"'Lady, I seek one favor, though I be a stranger, and have no claim to your regard, yet I have the boldness to prefer my request, having no greater desire than to live and die in your service. Let me then have your permission to try another fall with Mareguano; ay, and *another*, and *another*, even to a hundred, till he is satisfied of my superiority; for here striving in your presence, I know I am certain to come off with greater and greater glory in every trial.'

"And I, who cared little about the matter, carelessly granted what he asked.

"On the instant the two darted off to

meet each other: then came a prolonged struggle, fought out with desperate resolve; now lithely bending, now strained to their utmost height, they wrestled for a long space, grasping each other in such iron fashion that it would seem they scarce could breathe; at last the stranger youth ended the contest by seizing Mareguano round the body, then lifting him high in the air, and flinging him headlong on the ground.

"No sooner had he accomplished the feat than the assembled people, delighted at this exhibition of manly strength, bore him along in triumph to receive his reward at my hand.

"When I looked at him, kneeling before me again, flushed with success, praised and applauded by all around, yet waiting for my word, as if he prized it more than all the rest, I felt a new emotion take possession of me,—I perceived an interest in him which I had never experienced for any of the others, and it was with difficulty I could command myself sufficiently to conceal what I felt. However, I rose with all the dignity I could summon, placed the crown on his brow, and announced that the prize I held for the next contest was a ring ornamented with a fine emerald, and that it was for the winner in the race immediately to follow. I could not help saying it in such a way as to betray I expected it would be on *him* I should have to confer it. Nor was I mistaken.

"The competitors, forty in number, were

ranged in a long row, panting with anxiety to start. The signal scarcely given, the whole forty set off as one man, and so swiftly that their feet scarcely seemed to touch the sand; but Crepino (such was the name of the young stranger) pursued the sport with so much ardor that he distanced the very wind, and touched the red *Palio** before the others were near it. But I, when he was brought back to me, was more troubled than before; so that when I handed him the ring, I gave him as it were my liberty enclosed in it. And he no sooner had received the ring, than, holding it still before me, said,—

* *Palio*, a banner of bright-colored silk or cloth, hung across the end of the race-course among Spaniards, and given to the winner. Don Ercilla, all through the story, seems to fill up his incidents from Spanish manners and ideas.

"'*Señora*, I pray you accept it of me; for though it be but little to offer to you, yet it is offered with entire devotion, and the favor you will confer on me in accepting it will be so great, that it will make me rich, and shall so strengthen and animate me, that there will thenceforth be no undertaking so arduous that I shall not be able to accomplish it; and so you will have added the bravest heart and the stoutest arm to the Araucanian band.'

"I could not but accept what was so gracefully proffered; and now, the games being concluded, the meeting was broken up, and I had to return home with my father.

"For three weeks I concealed what I

felt, that I might not appear to change too suddenly from what had been a life-long resolve. But I could not overcome the desire to see him again. When next my father, therefore, urged me to make my choice among the young caciques, I told him that I had resolved to attend to his bidding, and that my choice had fallen on Crepino, who was of honorable name, brave, well-mannered, and well-grown.

"My father was all rejoiced at this announcement, and, kissing me on the forehead, he confirmed my choice; he told me how on Crepino of all the others his own heart yearned, and how Crepino himself had sued for me, and yet had urged him in no way to overrule my will.

"With joyful haste the nuptial ceremonies were performed over us, and all was mirth and gladness. That was but one short month ago, and to-day your people have slain him who was all my joy; and all our hopes of happiness are poured out like water on the ground. What comfort is there for so great misery! There is nothing left to hope for now, since earth contains no good which could be measured against such a grief!

"Now, therefore, let me seek my lord, and bury him; for it is not meet that his dear body should fall a prey to voracious beasts and birds."

Don Ercilla was so much moved by her recital that he no longer doubted her, but helped her to search for Crepino's body. When the morning dawned they found it, stark and cold, and disfigured by a cannon-ball. Tegualda's agony revived when she came in sight of his shattered form. She threw herself on him, placed her heart on his heart, and her lips on his, that so she might perchance yet call back the life; and then she struck her face, and tore her long dark hair, and pressed her fingers tightly round her throat, and threw herself again upon the ground, not knowing what she did for very grief. Don Ercilla looked on compassionating, knowing it was but distressing her to interfere till the first violence of her agony was past. Then, at peril of treachery toward him, alone in their midst, he bade her make a signal to call her people, and ordered them to bear away Crepino's body in decent order.

Then he composed her mantle round her, and, supporting her, gently led her along behind it till they reached the *sierra* where her own people dwelt, and then he delivered her over to her father's keeping.

ARAUCANIA.

III.

FITON'S CAVE.

DURING the course of the war an exploring party of Spaniards had been sent to bring a report of the chances of success to an expedition for recovering the coast-line of the Araucanian province, Time passed on, and the party failing to return, great anxiety was felt as to their fate by the Christians; at last some of the bravest volunteered to go and look after them in various directions, and as great caution was necessary, it was agreed the volunteers should go out separately, travelling by night, and keeping themselves concealed by day. It was a perilous enterprise, and Don Alonzo de Ercilla, who was always foremost at any brave deed, was the first to offer himself; and he gives us the following account of an adventure that befell him.

He was making his way through a wild brake, helped by the scanty light of the moon, when he found himself on the edge of a steep descent leading to a vast plain; a narrow path cut the steep, down which a tall, lank native of great age was threading his way. His back was bowed, he was so feeble that he trembled as he walked, and his legs were so fleshless that they looked like dry roots of trees. Don Ercilla advanced to offer his assistance down the rugged descent, and thought at the same time to gather some information of his missing friends, or as to the best means of tracing them. No sooner, however, was the old man conscious of his approach, than, darting into another path at a sharp angle with the first, he turned and fled up the steep side faster than a hunted deer. Don Ercilla spurred his horse, and thought to overtake him easily, but in a moment he was out of sight; neither was it possible for a stranger to find his way so as to proceed with any rapidity over the overgrown crag. Giving up the pursuit, he came at last to the bottom of the declivity, where the stream Rauco flowed turbulently, its course being closed in by sharp rocks on both sides; but a little way down it, on the near bank, was a grove of shady trees, and under them an antelope grazing. The sight reminded him he had once dreamt that this meeting an antelope should be a sign of something important to befall him, so, rejoicing at the incident, he made his way up to the gentle beast.

The antelope had been feeding undisturbed by the sound of the rushing torrent, but no sooner became conscious of a man's presence, than, leaving the verdant pasture, she struck wildly into a steep and narrow path, dashing through briar and jungle and close-grown trees; wherever she led, however, Don Ercilla followed, though he had need to spur his horse hard to keep up with her. At last she brought him in sight of a poor little hut, piled up at the foot of an ancient oak. At the sound of their hasty steps an old man came out, to whom, panting, the antelope approached as for protection. The old man tenderly stroked her reeking sides, and then, addressing Don Ercilla, asked him what fate or misadventure had brought him to his remote retreat, which strangers' steps had never yet found out. "If," he said, "you have had the misfortune to get separated from your company, you will find welcome here, and all that my humble roof can offer to restore strength; and fear nothing from your enemies while you are under my protection."

Finding him so affable and pleasant, Don Ercilla gave him his confidence, and not only told him his errand, but also opened to him a wish he had long harbored of visiting the cave of Fiton, the great Araucanian Wizard. The kind old man, without waiting so much as to answer him, took his hand, and at once leaving his seat set out to lead him. It was the season of early summer, and, as the sun was by this time well risen, they picked their way through the shadiest paths. As they went along, the old man spoke thus:—

"My lands were in Araucania. I am called Guaticolo the Unhappy, who, in my robust years, was a valiant fighting man, and in office predecessor to Colócolo.

Seven several times have I led our people on to victory on the battle-field, and a thousand times have my now hairless temples been girt with the tokens of success. But as in this life no state is permanent, so fortune was inconstant to me also. After success, came defeat; after honor, shame. At Aynavillo I had the misfortune to be loser in a wagered contest, on which my position had been set. Finding myself burdened with a dishonored life, I could devise no better end to it than to bury myself in this retreat, where, for twenty years, no mortal foot has tracked me; and by strange help it is, I ween, that you have been brought so far; who am I, therefore, to resist the direction you have received from above?

How intractable soever Fiton may be, I will urge the claims of relationship, as he is my uncle, and thus induce him to admit you.

"He dwells in the heart of a bleak mountain where the glad sun never penetrates, and whence the foot of man is shut out. But his wisdom and power are so great that he can by his one word perform any of nature's operations. In the blazing heat and dazzling light of noonday he can cover the heavens with the darkness of night. When the sky is one even blue, without assistance of wind or clouds, he can draw rain from a barren heaven. He can arrest the course of the bounding rivers, and of the birds in the midst of their flight. The burnt-up grasses of

August at his word raise their withered blades, and resume their verdant hues; the tides of the sea obey his voice, and forget the commands of the moon. And, much more than all this, he can tell the destinies of men, and foresee the fate of nations. It would be impossible for words of mine to overstate his mighty and irresistible power."

While he had been speaking they had passed through a long tract of forest, where the trees grew so thickly, and were so encumbered with brushwood, that Don Ercilla was obliged to tie his horse up and proceed on foot. At last they reached a low opening in a rock, through which was a long dark passage, where they could hardly walk upright, and at the end of it a door garnished all round with heads of wild beasts. Guaticolo opened the door, and led Don Ercilla by the hand into a spacious vault, in the centre of which burnt a strange and perpetual light; in the walls of the cave were cut many stone shelves, on which were ranged jars of ointments, essences, and herbs. There were preserved the far-piercing eyes of the lynx, and that of the venomous basilisk; red gore of angry men, and foam from the mouth of rabid dogs; parts of the wing of the harpy, the venom of the amphisbena, and the tail of the treacherous asp, which gives death wrapt up in a pleasant dream; mould off a truncated head unworthy of burial, and the tongue of the horrid hemorreo, whose puncture can never be staunched, but whosoever it wounds must bleed to death. In a huge transparent vase was a griffin's heart, pierced through with an arrow, and the ashes of an eastern phœnix. Stings of serpents, and tails of scorpions, and whatsoever is deadly and venomous in nature.

While Don Ercilla was engaged in examining this strange repertory, a hidden door gave entrance to a lean old man, whom he at once recognized for him who had run away from him with such exceeding rapidity, who said,—

"It is no little boldness in you, so young, to have dared to come thus unbidden to my presence, and to pursue me in my occult habitation, where it is not permitted to foot of man to tread; nevertheless, as

I know all things, I know that in your heart you mean no harm, therefore I allow you to live, and will now listen to your intent."

Then Guaticolo took upon himself to explain his errand for him in a long speech, in which he commenced by lauding the wizard's influence, then detailed Don Ercilla's fame, and finally told him of his dream, in which he had learnt that he might gain from Fiton supernatural information of the fate of the contest in which his Spanish brethren in arms were at the time engaged with the Turks in Europe.

Fiton, in great good humor with Guaticolo's dexterously-administered flattery, took Don Ercilla by the hand, and led him through the secret door by which he had himself entered. It opened into a very different apartment from the other. No mortal tongue could describe its beauty and costliness; the floor was paved with crystal tiles all lustrous with cunning radiance, while the roof was studded with brilliant stones, so that the whole place sparkled with dazzling splendor. Supported on pillars of shining gold, a hundred statues of heroes were ranged round the room, so life-like in design that a deaf man might have thought they spoke. On the broad medallions behind were pictured forth the valiant deeds of each, displaying the designer's acquaintance with the history of all nations.

In the midst of the spacious hall, which measured half a mile every way, swung a globe of light, balanced in the air by supernatural power.

When Don Ercilla had spent some time examining all these wonders, Fiton came to him, and, with his wand pointing to the globe of light, explained to him that it contained an epitome of the world, and had cost him forty years of labor; but contained the representation of all that was happening, or ever would happen, in any part or time of the world. "And," he added, "as it seems you are a poet, whose business it is to chronicle the great deeds of the fighting men of your country, and you have already celebrated their achievements by land, I will now show you what they are doing at sea."

Then he touched the bright globe with

his wand, and Don Ercilla saw it represented the world with all its parts delineated, and all the people on it seen as clearly as he might have seen his own face in a mirror.

Then Fiton pointed to the Mediterranean sea, and conducted his eyes to that part of it which washes* the Ausonian shore, and he saw it was all covered with galleys bearing the devices of the Pope, and Philip II., and the Venetian Republic; and from the port of Lepanto there came out to meet them the galleys of the Crescent. Then with a hoarse and terrible voice, Fiton invoked the infernal powers, crying, "O terrible Can-Cerberus, Charon, weary boatman, yellow Orcus, and irre-

* The Adriatic.

sistible Pluto! O chilly Styx, O lake Avernus, O seething waters of Acheron, Lethe, Cocytus, and ruddy Phlegethon! O Furies, who with relentless cruelty torment the souls of the lost, and Gorgons, whose hair of wriggling snakes the shades tremble as they behold! compelled by my all-powerful word, afford to this earth-born youth a clear vision of the work now accomplishing in the waters of Lepanto." As he spoke he frantically waved his wand.

Then behold, the waters of the sea boiled over, and the sterile north-east wind rounding the white sails, the rival fleets were tossed in sudden motion, the gallant Spanish vessels bearing down proudly on the Pagan galleys. Mighty warriors were there, whose names and deeds of fame were borne in characters of flame around their brows; some, whom he had known as companions of his own in childhood, now bronzed with the hardships of many a bold campaign. Suddenly the signal of the fight resounded, and then the Christian hosts, following the sign of their redemption, poured down with resistless ardor on their Pagan foes. With breathless interest Don Ercilla watched the fortunes of his friends, shouted to them—so present was the scene—to bear them bravely, nor waver in their courage. For hours the fight raged, and many a brave servant of Christ fell deadly wounded into the deep waves, and tinged the blue waters with his generous blood. Don Ercilla wept and exulted by turns, as, one after another, he saw dear friends lost to him forever in this life, and yet the Christian arms prevailing inch by inch, till at last, successful and triumphant, they swept the encroaching Turk from the face of the sea, inflicting an irreparable wound on his power, and setting a bound to his aggressions which he might not pass.

RAGUEL;

OR,

THE JEWESS OF TOLEDO.

ALFONSO VIII., King of Castile, succeeded to his throne in troublous times. His native country was overrun and subjugated by a people alien in nationality and religion, and his own particular dominions were a prey to civil dissensions, which had gathered strength during his minority. The Pope, Innocent III., seeing how he was beset, had called on other Christian nations to assist him in resisting the encroachments of the Moors; and these auxiliaries had unhappily shown themselves disorderly and rapacious, wasting the territory they had come to protect. By his prudence, Alfonso found the means to remedy all these disorders in turn. His French, German, and English allies, he dismissed to their own homes without involving himself in any quarrel with them. He established tolerable order and harmony among the rival families of the nobility, and he struck a blow against the Moors from which they never recovered, and which deserves to be remembered as one of the noblest achievements in the history of Christendom. After driving their hordes before him across the Sierra Morena, he gave them battle at a place called Las

Navas de Tolosa, undismayed by their overpowering numbers. During the early part of the day, it had seemed impossible to resist their countless hordes. "Father," said Alfonso, turning to the Archbishop of Toledo, "here are we called upon to lay down our life for the Faith." "Nay," answered the prelate, with almost prophetic instinct, "say, rather, here are we called to establish the triumph of the Faith." The cross-bearer, filled with ardor at the words, rushed into the thickest of the fray; the Christian soldiery hastened to protect the venerated sign, and so great was the enthusiasm which Alfonso's bravery kindled, that the infidel host was entirely routed, and its commander ran away into Africa.

Yet, notwithstanding his bravery and

his wisdom, Alfonso, like King Solomon of old, found it a harder matter to govern himself than to govern his kingdom; and though he had vanquished his adversaries, he suffered himself to be led away by his passions.

At Toledo, now a splendid ruin, then the magnificent capital of his kingdom, was a beautiful Jewish maiden, named Raguel, or Rachel, for whom he conceived a strong attachment. Now, the precepts alike of his religion and of his high position precluded his union with a Jewess and an obscure person, yet for all this he refused to part from her. The voice of the Archbishop, which had so notably animated his drooping spirits on the field of battle, was powerless with him now;

and he warned him in vain for seven years.

Mindful of the services he had rendered them, and for which they had awarded him the appellation of "the Noble," the people bore with the scandal all these years in silence, though with averted faces; but at last, when they found him gradually more and more unmindful of his former virtues, and all his prowess forgotten, that he might squander his time and his revenues on the fancies of the Jewish maiden, murmurs began to arise, and they determined to deliver their noble king from her enchantments.

Hernan García de Castro and Alvar Fañez, two of the highest nobles of Castile, were foremost in leading the resolve of the people, and urging it on the king. They had never failed his summons in the hour of danger, they had fought bravely by his side against their country's enemies, and their virtue and valor gave weight to their words. Yet the king was so tardy in attending to them that the people lost all patience.

The king was keeping his court in the sumptuous alcázar, the palatial fortress whose ruins even yet strike the traveller with admiration. Abandoning himself to the enjoyments of the delightful spot, Raguel and he sat one day, surrounded by their favorites and flatterers. "May divine Raguel's surpassing beauty ever continue to be the aurora of Toledo, ever enamel its brilliant sunlight!" said one of their minstrels, to the accompaniment of his joyous instrument.

"May she rejoice in her surpassing beauty as many ages are there are sands of gold* under the limpid torrent of crystal Tagus!" responded another.

Suddenly there burst on their affrighted ears the noise of a tumultuous gathering of people. The venal minions fled. The king, still worthy of himself, rose to show himself to his people, and Raguel was left alone to hear her sentence pronounced in ominous shouts from without:—

"Muera Raguel, para que Alfonso viva!"
"Rachel must die, that Alfonso may live!"

* The soil of the bed of the Tagus is a yellow sand, which gives its water rather a muddy appearance. Poets, however, see things with a different eye from ordinary mortals, and have turned it into gold in their verses: "el dorado Tajo," the goldon Tagus, is their common appellation for it.

García de Castro stood between the king and his angry people. The king called him a traitor; and he knelt and laid his sword at his feet, offering willingly to receive sentence of death if he could be proved a traitor, but insisting on being heard first. He then exposed to the king the wrongs of which his people complained. He asked him of what use were all the laurels he had gathered in the earlier part of his reign, if they were to be hung up to wither out of sight.

"Corn cannot ripen if the sun withhold its rays, flowers will not flourish if the gardener neglect to water them, neither can the Castilian people prosper if their king hide himself from them." So well did the intrepid García plead the right cause, that the king, overcome by his righteous arguments, promised to be himself again, to dismiss Raguel, and live once more for his subjects.

Delighted with his promise, the people returned peaceably to their homes.

The king, however, was not so strong as he thought. He imagined he had conquered himself, and went to take leave of Raguel. But the beautiful Jewess had no idea of letting him off so easily. Decked in her most captivating attire, she came out to meet him, and with her graces and tears succeeded so well in undermining his determination, that his promise was forgotten; and, like the phœnix from its ashes, Raguel rose more powerful than ever, and more dangerous too, for now a struggle had begun between her and the people—one or the other must be vanquished.

Infatuated by her entreaties, the king went so far as to place her on the throne. The indignation of the Castilians at seeing a low-born Jewess on the ancient seat of their monarchs, can scarcely be conceived; but it overflowed all bounds, when decree after decree went forth, heaping taxes on the Christian population and exemptions on the Jews—when proscriptions and executions of the highest in the land were threatened, and the noble García himself was sent into exile.

In this last step Raguel had outwitted herself. García gone, there was no one to act as moderator of the people. They rose in mass and stormed the palace; assembling in the basilica, they solemnly pronounced her worthy of death as an enemy of their king and country, and with desperate resolve drew their swords and turned to execute their award on the spot.

The king was absent on a hunting expedition; but García, who had heard of the new rising of the people, risked his life by infringing the sentence of banishment in order to save the life of his persecutor.

He succeeded in reaching her before the people had made their way into her apartment, and telling her of her danger, urged her to fly. But, loth to lose her high position, she refused, calling on her guards to defend her. The Castilian guards, however, refused to draw on their countrymen in defense of a Jewess. Meantime the people streamed in, and rushed upon her.

"Stay," said García; "stain not the bright steel of your Toledan blades with blood which belongs only to the sword of the executioner."

And his voice acted for a moment like the spell upon them.

But they were determined not again to leave it in her power to trample on their ancient institutions, and once more turned to slay her.

Then Alva Fañez drew from his hiding-place behind the throne a trembling Jew, who had been Raguel's minister in her elevation, but had not the courage to defend her now, and compelled him to be her executioner.

The king, hastily recalled from the chase, arrived but in time to see her expire. In the first burst of grief and fury he would have steeped his sword deep in the blood of his subjects; but once more the good García interposed, and by his temperate counsels recalled him to reason. When the violent throbbing of his agony had subsided, he acknowledged that his people had acted as a wise surgeon, that he alone had been in fault, that his punishment was deserved, and once more he was hailed as

ALFONSO EL NOBLE.

FINIS.

www.ingramcontent.com/pod-product-compliance
Lightning Source LLC
Chambersburg PA
CBHW032148160426
43197CB00008B/826